i

Newton Knew Biomechanics:
Unravel the Science Behind Human Movement by Beverly Simmons

Edited by Alex Wayne Stripling, Jr.

Published by Printing Futures, Vancouver, WA Copyright 2024 by Beverly

Simmons. All rights reserved.

Press. ISBN 978-1-942357- 61-2

Paperback Edition 2

Photo permissions from authors, illustrators, designers, and photographers are available for download at the URL. http://www.PrintingFutures.com

Newton Knew Biomechanics:
Unravel the Science Behind Human Movement

Contents

Dedicated to my three children, who are all grown now. They share my passions, pleasures, and problems with unconditional love and resilience, and to Hannah who inspires me to share my stories.

Meet a Passionate Educator

Beverly Simmons, a dedicated mother of three from a small town in southern GA, embarked on an inspiring journey to forge a fulfilling career in education and beyond. As a visionary and award-winning classroom teacher, she defied norms by creating an acclaimed program that integrated subjects in a multi-aged setting using data and analysis of project-based learning. Beverly and her ground-breaking team employed innovative ideas such as using racing and remote-control cars to teach core subjects while innovating using computer-based mathematics to teach algebra years before this technology was commonplace in schools. Beverly's accomplishments earned her a place among STEM Connector's prestigious inaugural 100 Women Leaders in STEM. Beverly also became a US State Department STEM speaker, and she has provided keynotes and professional development across the US and internationally.

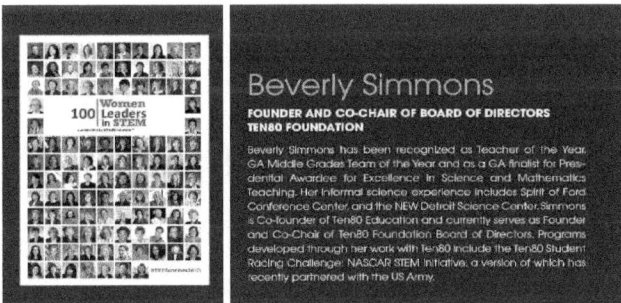

Beverly Simmons

FOUNDER AND CO-CHAIR OF BOARD OF DIRECTORS
TEN80 FOUNDATION

Beverly Simmons has been recognized as Teacher of the Year, GA Middle Grades Team of the Year and as a GA finalist for Presidential Awardee for Excellence in Science and Mathematics Teaching. Her informal science experience includes Spirit of Ford Conference Center, and the NEW Detroit Science Center. Simmons is Co-founder of Ten80 Education and currently serves as Founder and Co-Chair of Ten80 Foundation Board of Directors. Programs developed through her work with Ten80 include the Ten80 Student Racing Challenge: NASCAR STEM Initiative, a version of which has recently partnered with the US Army.

Preface

Biomechanics is a multidisciplinary field combining principles from physics, engineering, and biology. It focuses on investigating how internal and external forces influence the human body, aiming to unravel the intricacies of human movement.

Biomechanics' applications span a broad spectrum, encompassing the harmonious functioning of muscles and joints that drive human propulsion, optimizing sports performance, and advancing prosthetic technologies. Pursuing a degree in biomechanics opens diverse career avenues, allowing you to blend your enthusiasm for human movement, sports, and science to make a meaningful difference in people's lives.

With the potential for a competitive salary, you can significantly impact others by aiding athletes in achieving their best, innovating life-changing technologies for individuals with disabilities, or enhancing workplace ergonomics to boost productivity. A biomechanical career provides opportunities to contribute meaningfully to various aspects of people's lives.

Chapter 1: Introduction to Biomechanics

What is Biomechanics?

Biomechanics is a fascinating field of study that aims to understand and explain the mechanics of human movement. It combines principles from physics, engineering, and biology to analyze how external forces and internal mechanics interact to influence how our bodies move. In the subchapter titled "What is Biomechanics?", we will delve into the essence of this discipline, providing teachers training to teach Physical Science to middle and high school students with an overview of biomechanics and its relevance to forces and motion in the human body.

Biomechanics focuses on analyzing forces and motion in relation to the human body. By studying the mechanical properties of bones, muscles, tendons, and joints, biomechanists can understand how these structures work together to produce movement. They investigate how external forces, such as gravity and friction, affect our movements and how we can optimize our performance and minimize the risk of injury.

Biomechanics is divided into two main areas: statics and dynamics. Statics analyzes objects at rest or in equilibrium, while dynamics focuses on objects in motion. In the context of the human body, static biomechanics investigates posture, balance, and stability. In contrast, dynamic biomechanics explores the forces and motion involved in walking, running, jumping, and throwing activities.

Teachers can use biomechanics to engage their students in understanding the mechanics of the human body's movements. By introducing basic concepts like force, velocity, acceleration, and momentum, teachers can help students appreciate how these principles apply to everyday activities. Furthermore, studying biomechanics fosters an understanding of the science behind human movement and encourages critical thinking and problem-solving skills.

Biomechanics is an interdisciplinary field that explores how forces and motion affect the human body's movements. By understanding the principles of biomechanics, teachers can effectively teach Physical Science to middle and high school students, providing them with the knowledge and skills to analyze and optimize their movements. This subchapter introduces the fundamental concepts of biomechanics, laying a solid foundation for further exploration of forces and motion in biomechanics.

Importance of Biomechanics

Biomechanics is a fascinating field of study that examines the mechanics of human movement. It provides valuable insights into how forces and motion affect those movements.

One of the primary reasons why biomechanics is essential in understanding human movement is its practical application. By studying biomechanics, teachers can help students understand how forces and motion impact daily activities and sports performance. For example, biomechanics can explain the optimal technique for throwing a ball, the physics behind a basketball player's jump shot, or the mechanics of a gymnast's balance beam routine.

By understanding these principles, coaches can effectively teach their students the correct techniques and improve their performance in various physical activities.

Furthermore, biomechanics is crucial in preventing injuries and enhancing physical performance. By understanding the forces acting on the body during different movements, students learn how to reduce the risk of injuries. For instance, understanding the proper body mechanics when lifting heavy objects can prevent back injuries. Similarly, knowledge of biomechanics can help students improve their athletic performance by optimizing their movements and reducing the risk of strain or overuse injuries.

Biomechanics also provides a scientific framework for analyzing and evaluating movement, identifying strengths and weaknesses, and thinking more scientifically about human movement.

Finally, biomechanics can inspire students to pursue careers in related fields such as sports science, physical therapy, or biomechanical engineering. By introducing students to the exciting world of biomechanics, teachers can ignite a passion for scientific inquiry and discovery, opening doors to future opportunities.

To summarize, understanding the importance of biomechanics in understanding human movement is crucial for teachers training to teach Physical Science to middle and high school students. By incorporating biomechanics into their lessons, teachers can provide students with practical knowledge, prevent injuries, enhance performance, develop critical thinking skills, and inspire future careers. Forces and motion in biomechanics are captivating topics that can engage students and foster a lifelong interest in the science behind human movement.

Overview of the Book

Welcome to "Newton Knew Biomechanics: Unravel the Science Behind Human Movement." This book is part of the NEWTON KNEW Series, specifically designed for teachers training to teach Physical Science to middle and high school students interested in delving into the fascinating world of biomechanics. Biomechanics studies the mechanical principles that govern the human body's movement. It combines principles From physics, engineering, and biology to understand how forces and motion impact how we move. By exploring this field, teachers can help students develop a deeper understanding of the complex mechanisms that underlie human motion.

In the book's first part, we lay the foundation by introducing fundamental concepts of biomechanics. We explain the principles of force, motion, and energy and how they relate to the human body. We delve into Newton's laws of motion, friction, and the different forces acting on our bodies.

The book's second part focuses on applying biomechanics to specific movements. We explore how forces and motion affect walking, running, jumping, and throwing. Through interactive activities, experiments, and real-life examples, we provide teachers with valuable tools to engage students in hands-on learning experiences.

Moreover, we address common misconceptions and challenges students may encounter when studying biomechanics. We offer guidance on presenting complex concepts in an accessible and engaging manner, ensuring that students grasp the underlying principles while fostering their curiosity and critical thinking skills.

Finally, we provide teachers with various resources to enhance their teaching. We include lesson plans, worksheets, and assessment tools that align with educational standards, making it easier for teachers to integrate biomechanics into their physical science curriculum.

"Newton Knew Biomechanics: Unravel the Science Behind Human

Movement" is a comprehensive guide that equips teachers with the knowledge and tools to teach biomechanics effectively. By engaging students in the study of forces and motion in biomechanics, we aim to inspire the next generation of scientists and engineers while fostering a deeper understanding of the human body's incredible capabilities.

Chapter 2: Forces and Motion in Human Movement

Types of Forces Acting on the Human Body

In the field of biomechanics, understanding the different types of forces that act on the human body is crucial to comprehending how our movements are influenced. This subchapter delves into the various forces at play and their effects on the human body. It aims to train teachers to teach physical science to middle and high school students with the knowledge to explain forces and motion in biomechanics effectively.

Firstly, gravity is a force that constantly acts upon the human body. It pulls us towards the Earth, giving weight to our bodies. Without gravity, we would float weightlessly. This force is especially significant in jumping, running, and balance, where the body's interaction with the ground is essential.

Another force that affects the human body is the ground reaction force (GRF). When we walk or run, our feet exert a force on the ground, and the ground, in turn, exerts an equal and opposite force on our feet. This force allows us to propel ourselves forward and maintain balance while moving. Understanding the concept of ground reaction force helps explain why specific movements and postures are more stable than others.

Friction is yet another force influencing the human body. It is the resistance encountered when two surfaces rub against each other. Friction is vital in preventing slipping or sliding during various activities, such as walking or gripping objects. Teachers must teach students the significance of friction and how it affects the body's ability to perform different movements safely.

Forces can also be classified as internal or external. Internal forces are generated within the body, such as muscles contracting to move. External forces, on the other hand, come from outside the body and act upon it. Examples of external forces include a push or pull from an external object or the force of impact during a collision.

Understanding the distinction between internal and external forces is crucial in analyzing how the body responds to different stimuli.

Fundamental Concepts: Newton's Laws of Motion

Sir Isaac Newton's Laws of Motion is one of the most significant contributions to physics and biomechanics. These laws form the foundation for understanding the forces that act upon the human body and how they affect our movements.

Newton's first law of motion, also known as the law of inertia, states that an object at rest tends to stay at rest, and an object in motion tends to stay in motion unless acted upon by an external force. This law is especially relevant when considering the human body's movements.

For instance, when a person stands still, gravity acts upon them, keeping them grounded. When they start walking or running, the force exerted by their muscles overcomes the inertia, propelling them forward. This law applies to both linear and rotational motion. It describes the tendency of objects to maintain their state of motion (or rest) unless an external force is applied.

The second law of motion explains the relationship between force, mass, and acceleration. It states that the acceleration of an object is directly proportional to the net force acting on it and inversely proportional to its mass. In biomechanics, this law helps teachers explain how the human body accelerates and decelerates during various activities. For example, when a person jumps, the force exerted by their leg muscles propels them into the air. The greater the force and the lighter the body, the higher the jump.

This law is a fundamental equation for both linear and angular (rotational) motion. For linear motion, it is often expressed as F=ma, where F is force, m is mass, and a is acceleration. In rotational motion, the law involves torque (τ), moment of inertia (I), and angular acceleration (α).

Newton's third law of motion states that for every action, there is an equal and opposite reaction. This law is particularly relevant in understanding the biomechanics of walking and running. When a person steps forward, the ground exerts an equal and opposite force backward, propelling them forward. Similarly, when a person pushes against a wall, the wall exerts an equal force back on them, preventing them from moving through it.

This law is also applicable to both linear and angular motion. In linear motion, it implies that when one object exerts a force on a second object, the second object exerts an equal and opposite force on the first. In rotational motion, the law applies to torques, stating that there is an equal and opposite torque for every torque exerted. Fundamental physics determines the biomechanics of walking, running, jumping, and other physical activities.

Newton's laws of motion are simple to state, and sometimes teachers mistake the ability of students to recite the three laws correctly as evidence that they understand them. The fact that it took such a long time, historically, to codify the laws of motion suggests that they are not self-evident truths, no matter how obvious they may seem to us once we understand them well.

Much research in recent years has documented that students typically have trouble relating formal ideas of motion and force to their personal view of how the world works. As indicated earlier, the basic idea expressed in Newton's second law of motion is not difficult to grasp. Still, vocabulary may get in the way if students struggle over the meaning of force and acceleration. Both terms have many meanings in everyday language that confuse their specialized use in science.

These are three of the obstacles:

1. A fundamental problem is the ancient perception that sustained motion requires sustained force. The contrary notion that it takes force to change an object's motion, that something in motion will move in a straight line forever without slowing down unless a force acts on it, runs counter to what we can see happening with our eyes.

2. Limitations in describing motion may keep students from learning about the effect of forces. Students of all ages tend to think in terms of motion or no motion. So, the first task may be to help students divide the category of motion into steady motion, speeding up, and slowing down. For example, falling objects should be described as falling faster and faster rather than just falling.

3. Like inertia, the action-equals-reaction principle is counterintuitive. To say that a book presses down on the table is sensible enough, but then to say that the table pushes back up with the same force (which disappears the instant you pick up the book) seems false on the face of it. What is to be done? Students should have lots of experiences to shape their intuition about motion and forces long before encountering laws. Especially helpful are experimentation and discussion of what happens as surfaces become more elastic with less friction. (Benchmarks in Science Literacy)

This classroom lesson is an example of how the idea of Newton's laws and humans in motion might be introduced in a classroom setting. The lesson uses the 5 E format: Engage, Explore, Explain, Evaluate, Extend.

Lesson Plan
Newton's 1st Law Applied to Human Movements

ENGAGE:

Objective: Introduce the concept of inertia and Newton's First Law of Motion through a relatable and engaging activity.

Activity: "Human Tug-of-War"
Divide the students into two teams. Each team holds a rope, and they engage in a tug-of-war. After a brief round, ask students to reflect on what they observed during the game, emphasizing that objects (or people) at rest tend to stay at rest.

Examples of "Human Tug-of-War" Observations
Initial Resistance: At the start of the tug-of-war, students will notice that both teams experience resistance as they try to move the rope in their direction. This resistance represents the initial state of rest or equilibrium.

Difficulty in Stopping: Once a team manages to start pulling the rope in their direction, students will observe that it is challenging for the opposing team to stop the motion. Objects in motion tend to stay in motion.

Change in Motion: If one team successfully pulls the other, students will see a change in motion, and the team in motion continues until an external force (the other team pulling harder) acts on it.

Discussion Points:

- Introduction to Inertia: Begin by discussing the term "inertia." Explain that inertia is the tendency of an object to resist changes in its state of motion— whether at rest or in motion.
- Objects at Rest: Discuss the initial resistance observed when both teams are at rest, relating it to the concept that objects at rest tend to stay at rest unless acted upon by an external force.
- Objects in Motion: Emphasize the difficulty in stopping the motion once it starts, highlighting that objects in motion tend to stay in motion unless acted upon by an external force.
- Newton's First Law Connection: Connect the observations to aw of Motion. Explain that the tug-of-war scenario exemplifies how objects (teams in this case) at rest stay at rest until a force (pulling) is applied, and objects in motion stay in motion until another force (opposing team's pull) acts on them.
- Real-Life Applications: Relate the tug-of-war activity to real-life situations, such as a car at a stoplight or a person on a bike. Discuss how these examples align with the principles of inertia and Newton's First Law. By anchoring the explanation in the observations made during the "Human Tug-of-War," students can better grasp the concept of inertia and Newton's First Law of Motion in the context of human movements.

EXPLORE Objective: Allow students to experience inertia firsthand and understand the concept through exploration. Activity: "Inertia Stations" Set up stations with various inertia-related activities. Each Station should have observation sheets or cards. These are a few examples.

- Station 1: Rolling Ball Activity
- Station 2: Chair on Wheels
- Station 3: Pendulum Swing
- Station 4: Spinning Top
- Station 5: Hovercraft Ride
- Station 6: Air-Powered Car

Station 1: Rolling Ball
Activity: Place a smooth surface (like a table or a board) at an incline. Have students release a small ball at the top of the incline and observe its motion.
Object Used: [Ball]

Observations:
- Describe the motion of the ball as it rolls down the incline.
- What happens when there are no obstacles in the ball's path?
- Does the ball stop on its own or require an external force?
- Make any other observations related to the ball's motion.

Station 2: Chair on Wheels
Activity: Place a chair with wheels on a smooth surface. Ask students to push the chair and observe its motion.
Object Used: [Chair with Wheels]

Observations:
- Describe how the chair moves when pushed
- What happens when there are no obstacles in the ball's path?
- Does the chair come to a stop immediately or continue moving?
- Notice any differences in motion compared to the rolling ball.

Station 3: Pendulum Swing
Activity: Set up a pendulum by suspending a heavy object (e.g., a weight or a pendulum bob) from a string. Ask students to release the pendulum from the starting position and observe its swing.
Object Used: [Pendulum]

Observations:
- Describe the motion of the pendulum as it swings.
- Does the pendulum eventually come to a stop on its own?
- How does the pendulum behave when stopped by a hand?
- Patterns or observations related to the pendulum's motion.

Station 4: Spinning Top

Activity: Provide students with spinning tops. Instruct them to spin the tops on a flat surface and observe their behavior.
Object Used: [Spinning Top]

Observations:
- Describe how the top behaves when spinning.
- Does the top eventually stop spinning on its own?
- What happens if an external force, like a finger, stops the top?
- Any peculiar motions or patterns observed.

Station 5: Hovercraft Ride

Activity: Set up a skateboard on a smooth surface. Ask students to give it a gentle push and observe its motion.
Object Used: [Hovercraft or Skateboard]

Observations:
- Describe the Hovercraft's motion when pushed.
- How does the Hovercraft come to a stop?
- What happens if there is no obstacle in its path?
- Note differences or similarities compared to other activities.

Station 6: Air Powered Car

Activity: Provide students with balloon-powered toy cars. Ask them to inflate the balloon and then release the air to propel the car.
Object Used: [Balloon-Powered Car]

Observations:
- Describe the motion of the car when the balloon is released.
- How does the car come to a stop?
- Does the car's motion change if the surface is altered?
- Other interesting observations related to the balloon car.

EXPLAIN

Objective: Explain Newton's First Law of Motion and how it applies to human movements.

Teaching Strategy: Start with a brief discussion on the observations from the exploration activities. Introduce Newton's First Law: An object at rest stays at rest, and an object in motion stays at the same speed and direction unless acted upon by an unbalanced external force. Discuss how this law applies to their activities during the "Human Tug-of-War" and "Inertia Stations."

EVALUATE

Objective: Assess student understanding of Newton's First Law. Pose questions to the students, such as: "What is Newton's First Law of Motion?" "How does inertia relate to the activities we did today?" "Can you give an example of Newton's First Law in your daily life?"

EXTEND

Objective: Apply understanding to real-life scenarios. Extension Activity: "Everyday Inertia"- Assign a homework task where students observe and document for discussion instances of inertia in their daily lives (e.g., a car coming to a stop, a soccer ball rolling to a halt).

Chapter 3: Center of Mass and Stability

Understanding the concept of center of mass and stability in biomechanics is crucial when studying how forces and motion affect the human body's movements. The center of mass refers to the point within an object where its mass is evenly distributed. It is the balance point of an object, and in the human body, it plays a significant role in maintaining stability during various activities and movements.

For teachers training to teach Physical Science to middle and high school students, explaining the concept of center of mass and stability can be challenging. However, students can grasp these fundamental concepts more effectively by breaking them down into simpler terms and using relatable examples.

When it comes to the human body, the center of mass is generally located around the belly button area because most of our mass is concentrated in the trunk region. By understanding this, students can comprehend how the center of mass affects their balance and stability during everyday activities.

To illustrate this point, teachers can engage their students in activities such as balancing on one leg or walking on a balance beam.

By challenging their center of mass and stability, students can experience firsthand how a slight shift in their body position can affect their balance and stability. This practical approach allows students to connect the theoretical concept to their own bodies and movements.

Moreover, teachers can introduce the idea of stability by explaining how a broader support base can enhance stability. For instance, when standing with feet shoulder-width apart, the base of support is broader, making it easier to maintain balance. Conversely, standing with feet close together reduces the support base, and maintaining stability is more challenging.

The center of mass (COM) is a point in an object or system where its mass is concentrated. In human movement, the center of mass plays a crucial role in maintaining balance and stability. Here are several examples of how the center of mass affects human movement:

Walking and Running: During walking and running, the center of mass moves rhythmically. The body adjusts its position relative to the ground to maintain stability. The horizontal movement of the center of mass contributes to the forward propulsion during each step.

Effect on Balance: By leaning slightly forward, individuals can position their center of mass ahead of their feet, facilitating forward motion. The control of the center of mass is essential for maintaining balance and preventing falls during these dynamic activities.

Balancing on One Leg: When standing on one leg, the center of mass must be directly above the supporting foot to maintain balance. The body shifts the position of the center of mass over the base of support to prevent tipping.

Precision and Grace: Athletes, dancers, or individuals in activities like yoga often practice balancing on one leg. Controlling the center of mass allows for graceful movements and precise control over body positioning.

Diving Board Jump: Individuals adjust their body position on a diving board to ensure their center of mass aligns with the board's axis. This alignment influences the trajectory of the jump.

Position: By controlling the position of their center of mass, a diver can execute spins, flips, and twists with precision. The movement of the center of mass determines the rotation and orientation during the jump.

Skiing Downhill: While skiing downhill, individuals shift their weight and adjust the position of their center of mass to maintain stability and control speed. Leaning into turns helps initiate and guide the direction of the skis.

Turns and Terrain: Manipulating the center of mass is critical for carving turns and navigating varied terrain. Skiers use their body position to distribute weight over the skis effectively.

Figure Skating Spin: During a spin in figure skating, the skater pulls their arms and legs inward, bringing their body's mass closer to the rotation axis. This action decreases the moment of inertia, facilitating faster spins.

Moment of Inertia: Controlling the center of mass and moment of inertia is essential for achieving impressive spins. Skaters extend their bodies to slow down spins and bring them in to increase rotational speed.

Gymnastics Balance Beam Routine: Gymnasts performing on the balance beam carefully adjust their center of mass over the narrow surface to maintain balance. Movements involve controlled shifts to prevent falls.

Effect on Control: Precise control of the center of mass allows gymnasts to execute complex routines on the balance beam. They use subtle adjustments to stay aligned with the beam and perform intricate skills.

Overall, the center of mass and stability are integral components in biomechanics, and understanding their significance allows individuals to analyze and appreciate the intricate workings of the human body's movements. This knowledge can further serve as a foundation for exploring more complex biomechanical principles, such as the role of the center of mass in sports performance or the importance of stability in physical rehabilitation.

Here is an example of how the idea of Newton's laws and humans in motion might be introduced in a classroom setting.

Lesson Plan
Exploring the Center of Gravity with Paper Towers

ENGAGE:
Objective: Introduce the concept of center of gravity by relating it to the stability of 1/10th scale cars and their performance on curves.

Activity: Discuss the importance of the center of gravity in cars, especially in racing situations. Show images or diagrams of cars with different heights and ask students to consider the role of the center of gravity regarding stability. Discuss the impact of the center of gravity on the behavior of cars when turning corners and the use of roll bars. Relate the laws of physics governing car stability to a hands-on activity with paper towers.

EXPLORE:
Objective: Allow students to explore the concept of center of gravity through a hands-on activity—building paper towers
Exploration Activity: "Paper Tower Challenge"

- Divide students into small groups (2-3 students per group). Provide each group with a sheet of paper (20-25 lb. wt.).
- Challenge: Build the tallest free-standing tower possible without using tape or glue.
- Set a minimum height requirement (e.g., 50 cm) before they can conclude the activity.
- After the first attempt, encourage students to share ideas and strategies with other groups.

EXPLAIN:
Objective: Explain the relationship between tower height, center of gravity, and stability.

Discuss the results of the tower-building activity as a class. Explore questions such as: "What happened to the center of gravity as you added height to the tower?" "How did the tower's balance change with increasing height?" "Could you add more mass to the bottom to lower the center of gravity and increase stability?"

EVALUATE:
Objective: Assess students' understanding of center of gravity and its impact on stability.

Assessment: Ask students to reflect on their tower-building experience and answer questions like:

- How did the center of gravity influence the balance of your tower?"
- Could adding more mass at the bottom have improved stability?
- Relate the tower experiment to the center of gravity in cars. How might this impact performance?

EXTEND:
Objective: Extend the concept of center of gravity to real-world scenarios, particularly in racing and vehicle dynamics.

Extension Activity: "Car Center of Gravity Simulation" Discuss different racing scenarios (banked track, flat curve, drag strip) and how the center of gravity influences car performance. Challenge students to simulate the impact of changing the center of gravity on a model car and observe its effects on speed and stability. Discuss the practical implications of adjusting the center of gravity in racing.

Torque and Moment of Inertia

The concept of moment of inertia is closely related to torque. It measures how difficult it is to change an object's rotational motion. Just as mass measures an object's resistance to linear motion, moment of inertia measures an object's resistance to rotational motion.

Torque refers to the rotational force that causes an object to rotate around an axis. On the other hand, the moment of inertia measures an object's resistance to changes in its rotational motion.

Stated simply, torque is the force that causes an object to twist or rotate. When we apply force to an object, such as pushing or pulling on a lever, torque is produced.

This torque can be calculated by multiplying the force applied by the distance from the axis of rotation. Teachers training to teach Physical Science to middle and high school students can explain torque using relatable examples, such as opening a door or riding a bike.

When pedaling a bike, you apply force to the pedals, creating a torque around the axis of the bike's crank. The pedals are attached to the crank, which is connected to the bike's chainring, which is part of the bike's drivetrain.

The torque applied to the pedals results in the rotational motion of the crank, which, through the chain, eventually drives the bike's wheels. The length of the crank arm (the distance from the pedal attachment point to the axis of rotation) affects the torque applied to the drivetrain. Cyclists often adjust their gears to influence torque. Longer crank arms give you more leverage. This leverage can increase torque but might require more effort.

Conversely, a shorter crank arm might decrease torque and require less effort. A shorter crank arm enables you to keep up a higher cadence, which is why triathletes often prefer them.

The concept of moment of inertia is closely related to torque. It measures how difficult it is to change an object's rotational motion. Just as mass measures an object's resistance to linear motion, moment of inertia measures an object's resistance to rotational motion.

The moment of inertia depends on both the mass and the distribution of mass around the axis of rotation. Teachers can illustrate this concept using examples like a spinning figure skater pulling their arms in to increase their rotational speed.

Understanding torque and moment of inertia plays a significant role in analyzing and predicting human movement. For example, when performing exercises or sports activities, the torque generated by muscles and joints determines the speed and efficiency of the movement.

The moment of inertia of body segments influences the ease with which an individual can perform actions like jumping or spinning.

In each of these examples, the principles of torque and moment of inertia are crucial for understanding and controlling the rotational aspects of human body movements:

Diver in Mid-Air:
When a diver is in mid-air during a somersault or twist, they can control their rotation by adjusting their body position. By changing the distribution of their mass (moment arm) relative to their rotation axis, they can control the torque acting on their body.

The diver can tuck or spread their body to change their moment of inertia. Tucking decreases the moment of inertia, allowing for faster rotation, while spreading increases it, slowing down the rotation.

Gymnast on Rings:
Torque: A gymnast performing on rings must generate torque to initiate and control rotations. For example, when executing a dismount,

the gymnast extends their body to increase the moment arm, creating torque contributing to the rotation.

Controlling the position of the body parts, such as spreading or bringing together the legs, affects the moment of inertia. Adjusting the moment of inertia allows the gymnast to control the speed of the rotation.

Pole Vaulter Clearing the Bar:

A pole vaulter generates torque by applying force to the pole during takeoff. By pushing against the pole with their hands and bending it, they create a torque that helps lift their body over the bar.

The vaulter can control their body's moment of inertia by adjusting their position while clearing the bar. For instance, bringing their legs close to their body decreases the moment of inertia, aiding in rotational maneuvers.

Swimmer Performing a Flip Turn:

A swimmer executing a flip turn in freestyle or butterfly generates torque by pushing against the pool wall with their feet. The force applied at a distance from the body's rotation axis produces torque, facilitating the quick turn.

The swimmer can manipulate their moment of inertia during the flip turn by curling into a compact position, decreasing the moment of inertia and allowing for a faster rotation.

Martial Artist Executing a Spin Kick:

A martial artist generates torque during a spin kick by exerting force through the leg muscles. The rotational force applied at a distance from a body's center contributes to the spinning motion.

By extending or retracting their limbs during the spin, the martial artist can control their moment of inertia. A more extended position increases the moment of inertia, slowing the spin, while a compact position decreases it, allowing for faster rotation. Students can apply these concepts to analyze and evaluate various movements in sports, exercise, and everyday life. It is also important to understand that external forces exerted on the human body significantly influence linear and angular motion. Gravity, friction, air resistance, and other applied forces impact the body's movement patterns. For instance, demonstrating the impact of air resistance on a person running at different speeds can help students understand the role of external forces in shaping human movement.

Projectile Motion: Analyzing Trajectories

One fascinating aspect of this field is projectile motion, which involves analyzing the trajectories of human movements. Projectile motion refers to the path followed by an object launched into the air and then subject only to the force of gravity and air resistance. Regarding human movements, numerous activities can be analyzed through the lens of projectile motion, such as throwing a ball, kicking a soccer ball, or even jumping.

By examining these movements, students can gain insights into the factors that affect the trajectory of an object. They can explore concepts like initial velocity, angle of projection, and air resistance, all of which play significant roles in determining the path of a projectile. For instance, students can investigate how changing the angle of a soccer ball kick affects its trajectory or how air resistance alters the flight path of a thrown object.

Understanding projectile motion can also highlight the importance of skill and precision in various sports and activities. For instance, the angle and force with which a player shoots the ball in basketball determines whether it reaches the basket. Similarly, in the long jump, athletes must consider their angle of projection to achieve optimal distance. Moreover, analyzing the trajectories of human movements can help students appreciate how simple adjustments in body position can alter an outcome.

Spotlight on Baseball

In sports, a revolutionary transformation is underway, with biomechanics emerging as a game-changer.

This transformation is particularly evident in baseball, where cutting-edge technologies are reshaping how athletes approach their game. In pursuing excellence, players willingly subject themselves to the intricacies of biomechanical analysis, a process that demands vulnerability and discomfort.

The journey into the heart of biomechanics begins with a meticulous motion capture process. Athletes, clad in nothing more than their essentials, find themselves under the scrutiny of high-tech cameras and sensors. The discomfort is tangible, but so is the commitment to unlocking the secrets of optimal performance.

In this immersive process, players throw, swing, and move in ways that transcend traditional metrics. The story unfolds against a shift from output-focused metrics to an exploration of inputs — a quest to understand what players achieve and how they do it.

The narrative refers to the 1980s when the seeds of biomechanical analysis were planted. Technological innovations, such as high-speed cameras and algorithms, paved the way for the first wave of biomechanical insights in the 1990s. A pivotal moment in this narrative is the advent of markerless motion capture, a breakthrough that liberates athletes from the constraints of laboratory settings.

This technology, exemplified by Kinatrax, propels biomechanics into a new frontier, enabling three-dimensional data collection without the need for adhesive sprays and reflective markers. It signifies a shift from the lab to the field, from controlled conditions to the unpredictable dynamics of live games.

The heart of the story lies in applying biomechanics to player development. The analysis goes beyond mere outputs, providing a deep dive into how individual athletes move compared to their peers. It is a process of self-discovery, where players like Tristan Garnett of the Phillies acknowledge the discomfort but recognize the pursuit of scientific truth beneath it.

Corrective drills become the tools of transformation, personalized for each athlete based on their biomechanical assessments. The brilliance lies not only in the training process but in the ability of laboratories and teams to evaluate these drills for effectiveness rigorously.

This process departs from traditional player development, where precision was challenging, and improvement assessments were riddled with uncertainties. Yet, challenges abound in this biomechanical odyssey. The cost of advanced systems poses a hurdle, with only a fraction of teams investing in these technologies.

Integrating biomechanical data into coaching philosophies becomes a crucial bridge to cross. It is not just about acquiring data; it is about deciphering its meaning and seamlessly incorporating it into the fabric of player development.

The narrative explores the complexities of the following steps — from assessing inefficiencies to deciding whether to address them or acknowledge their role in a player's unique style. It delves into the dichotomy of improving player performance versus potential injury risks, underlining the thin line that coaches tread in pursuing performance optimization.

As the pages turn, the future of biomechanics in baseball emerges as an evolving landscape. The focus shifts from the installation of labs to the democratization of movement analysis, from acquiring data to understanding how to apply it optimally.

The story culminates in a vision where biomechanics and human movement data become as integral to sports as ball flight data. The spotlight is on the mysteries of biomechanics — linking pitcher movements to on-field results, decoding deception, and quantifying the unexpected. The journey is not just about numbers; it is about understanding physics, applying knowledge, and building a future where every player has access to the transformative power of biomechanics.

In the sports arena, where science meets athleticism, the less-than-comfortable journey into biomechanics is not just a chapter; it is a paradigm shift, shaping the future of how we understand and play the game.

The future — and present — of baseball is in biomechanics Eno Sarris and Alec Lewis Feb 25, 2022, 41

Chapter 4: Biomechanics of Walking and Running

Anatomy and Mechanics of Walking

Walking is a fundamental human movement that we often take for granted. However, understanding the anatomy and mechanics behind walking is essential for teachers training to teach Physical Science to middle and high school students. This subchapter will delve into the intricacies of the human body's movements during walking, shedding light on the forces and motion involved.

Let us first explore the anatomy of walking. The human body consists of various interconnected parts that work harmoniously to facilitate locomotion. The lower limbs play a crucial role, comprising the femur, tibia, fibula, and numerous smaller bones in the feet. Additionally, muscles, tendons, and ligaments work together to provide stability and enable movement.

To comprehend the mechanics of walking, it is important to understand the concept of a gait cycle. This cycle consists of two phases: stance and swing. During the stance phase, one foot is in contact with the ground while the other foot swings forward. This alternation allows for continuous movement. As the foot lands, it absorbs the impact through the complex interaction between bones, muscles, and joints.

The forces acting on the body heavily influence the mechanics of walking. Gravity plays a significant role during the gait cycle, as it pulls the body downward, affecting the distribution of forces. Teachers can explain to their students how the body's center of mass shifts during different stages of walking and how it affects stability.

Moreover, forces such as friction and air resistance also come into play. Friction acts between the foot and the ground, providing traction and preventing slipping. Air resistance, on the other hand, affects the body during the swing phase, when the foot is off the ground. Understanding these forces allows students to appreciate the complexity of walking.

Biomechanical Analysis of Running

Running is a fundamental human movement that is also a form of exercise and a competitive sport. When analyzing the biomechanics of running, several key factors come into play. The first is understanding the forces involved. Running is a dynamic activity that requires the application of forces to propel the body forward.

These forces include the ground reaction force, which is the force exerted by the ground on the body, and the muscular forces generated by the legs and core muscles.

Teachers should also explore the concept of motion in relation to running. Running involves a cyclic motion called the running gait cycle, which consists of the stance and swing phases. During the stance phase, the foot makes contact with the ground, and the body is supported by one leg. In the swing phase, the leg is in the air, moving forward to prepare for the next stance phase.

To further delve into the biomechanics of running, teachers can discuss the body's joint movements and muscle actions. The ankle, knee, and hip joints play crucial roles in transferring forces and generating motion during running.

Students should understand the actions of the quadriceps, hamstrings, and calf muscles in coordinating joint movements and reducing the necessary forces for running. By breaking down the biomechanics of running into these detailed components, students can understand how joint movements and muscle actions collaborate to produce efficient and effective running mechanics.

Joint Movements:

Ankle Joint:

Dorsiflexion and Plantarflexion:

The ankle joint undergoes dorsiflexion (foot lifting toward the shin) during the swing phase of running and plantarflexion (pointing the toes) during the push-off phase. These movements work together to produce effective propulsion.

Knee Joint:

Flexion and Extension:

The knee joint primarily experiences flexion (bending) during the swing phase and extension (straightening) during the push-off phase of running.

Hip Joint:

Flexion and Extension, Abduction, and Adduction:

The hip joint undergoes flexion and extension during the swing and push-off phases, respectively. Additionally, abduction (moving away from the body's midline) and adduction (moving toward the midline) play roles in stabilizing the hip during running.

Muscle Actions:

Quadriceps:

Role in Running:

The quadriceps, comprising four muscles at the front of the thigh, play a crucial role in knee extension during the push-off phase. They provide the necessary power for propelling the body forward.

Hamstrings:

Role in Running:

Located at the back of the thigh, the hamstring contributes to hip extension during the push-off phase, coordinating with the quadriceps to ensure a smooth and efficient running stride.

Calf Muscles (Gastrocnemius and Soleus):

Role in Running:

The gastrocnemius and soleus muscles in the calf are essential for ankle plantarflexion, providing the force needed to push off the ground. These muscles are particularly active during the latter part of the stance phase.

Coordination of Movements:

These muscles work in harmony. For instance, during the stance phase, the quadriceps and calf muscles work together to extend the knee and plantarflex the ankle, respectively, creating a powerful push-off.

For Teachers: Teachers can utilize visual aids, animations, or demonstrations to illustrate these joint movements and muscle actions. Practical activities, such as analyzing slow-motion videos of running, can help students observe and understand the biomechanics in action.

It is also important to address common running injuries and how biomechanics can contribute to their occurrence. Teachers can discuss how poor running mechanics, such as overpronation or excessive impact forces, can increase the risk of injuries like shin splints or stress fractures. By understanding the biomechanical factors that contribute to these injuries, students can learn how to prevent them and improve their running technique.

Efficiency and Performance in Walking and Running

Walking and running are fundamental human movements that are influenced by various factors affecting efficiency and performance. Biomechanics aims to unravel these factors and provide insights into how they impact walking and running mechanics.

Biomechanical Factors:

Body Alignment: Proper alignment of the body is essential for efficient walking and running. Maintaining a straight posture, engaging core muscles, and aligning the limbs appropriately optimize performance.

Muscle Strength and Flexibility: Strong and flexible muscles are vital for generating force and absorbing impact during walking and running. Regular strength training and stretching exercises improve muscle performance.

Footwear and Surface: The choice of footwear and the nature of the surface affect the mechanics of walking and running. Appropriate footwear provides adequate support and cushioning. Additionally, different surfaces, such as grass, concrete, or sand, impact efficiency and performance.

Stride Length and Frequency: The length and frequency of strides greatly influence the efficiency of walking and running. Athletes optimize stride length and frequency to achieve the desired speed and conserve energy.

Environmental Factors:

Temperature and Humidity: Environmental conditions such as temperature and humidity can affect performance during walking and running. It is important that walkers and runners learn to pay attention to proper hydration, warm-up exercises, and adapting to different weather conditions.

Altitude: Walking and running at high altitudes pose additional challenges due to reduced oxygen availability. Athletes are at a disadvantage if they compete at higher altitudes than they practice.

Psychological Factors:

Motivation and Mental Focus: Psychological factors, including motivation and mental focus, play a significant role in walking and running efficiency. It is important that walkers and runners develop techniques for maintaining motivation and focus during physical activities.

Skill Acquisition and Technique: Developing proper walking and running techniques and practicing them is crucial for optimizing movement efficiency.

Understanding the factors affecting efficiency and performance in walking and running is essential for making informed choices, optimizing movements, and improving overall physical performance.

Chapter 5: Biomechanics of Jumping and Landing

Principles of Jumping Mechanics

Jumping is a fundamental human movement that involves the coordinated action of various muscles, tendons, and bones. One of the key principles of jumping mechanics is the concept of force. When a person jumps, they exert a force against the ground, which then exerts an equal and opposite force that propels them upwards. This force, known as the ground reaction force, is crucial for generating the necessary momentum to overcome gravity and achieve vertical displacement. The force applied during jumping can be influenced by leg strength, body position, and technique.

Another important principle is the conservation of energy. During a jump, the body transfers potential energy to kinetic energy. As the individual squats down and prepares to jump, they store potential energy in their muscles and tendons. This potential energy is rapidly converted into kinetic energy as the person pushes off the ground and propels themselves into the air.

Proper technique, body positioning, and body mechanics are critical for maximizing jump height and minimizing the risk of injury. Students should be taught how to align their bodies correctly, engage the appropriate muscles, and coordinate their movements to generate optimal force and achieve efficient jumps. Educators can use video demonstrations or practical activities to help students understand and practice correct jumping mechanics and enable them to apply these principles to other activities and sports involving forces and motion.

Biomechanical Analysis of Vertical Jumping

In sports and athletics, the ability to jump vertically is often a defining factor in an athlete's success. Whether basketball players go for a slam dunk or volleyball players spike the ball, the vertical jump is a fundamental movement that requires a deep understanding of biomechanics.

What forces are at play during a vertical jump? When an athlete jumps, the ground exerts an upward force on their body known as the ground reaction force. This force propels the athlete into the air, overcoming the force of gravity. Understanding the mechanics of this force and its interaction with the human body is essential for comprehending the mechanics of jumping. Biomechanical analysis allows us to break down the movement into a vertical jump into its key components, such as takeoff, flight, and landing. Each phase's angles, velocities, and accelerations contribute to a successful jump.

One critical aspect of vertical jumping is the role of muscles. Muscles function as engines that generate the force and power of a jump, just as they do for running.

The primary muscles involved in a vertical jump include:
Quadriceps (Rectus Femoris, Vastus Lateralis, Vastus Medialis, Vastus Intermedius): These muscles, located at the front of the thigh, are crucial for knee extension, providing the initial push-off during the jump.

Hamstrings (Biceps Femoris, Semitendinosus, Semimembranosus): The hamstrings, located at the back of the thigh, play a role in hip extension and contribute to the push-off phase of the jump.

Gluteal Muscles (Gluteus Maximus, Gluteus Medius, Gluteus Minimus): The gluteal muscles are involved in hip extension, assisting in propelling the body upward during the jump.

Gastrocnemius and Soleus (Calf Muscles): These muscles, located in the calf, contribute to ankle plantarflexion and provide additional force during the push-off phase of the jump.

Coordination of Muscle Actions:

Before the actual jump, the muscles undergo eccentric contractions, lengthening while absorbing the force of the downward movement. The muscles then transition to concentric contractions, shortening to generate force during the upward phase of the jump. The quadriceps, hamstrings, and gluteal muscles work in a synchronized manner to extend the hips and knees, while the calf muscles contribute to ankle plantarflexion.

This coordinated effort produces a powerful upward force, propelling the body off the ground.

Biomechanical analysis reveals that the body transforms potential energy into kinetic energy during takeoff and flight. Understanding this energy transfer process and the principles of energy conservation connects biomechanics to the broader field of physics.

Finally, jumpers are trained to maximize the performance of an individual's vertical jumping ability. From plyometric exercises to strength training, these methods can help students optimize their biomechanical performance in vertical jumping. Plyometrics, also known as jump training or plyos, are exercises in which muscles exert maximum force in short intervals, aiming to increase power (speed-strength). This training focuses on learning to move from a muscle extension to a contraction in a rapid or "explosive" manner, such as in specialized repeated jumping. Plyometrics are primarily used by athletes, especially martial artists, sprinters, and high jumpers, to improve performance, and they are used in the fitness field to a much lesser degree. (Note 8)

How high can someone jump?

Jump height really depends on the technique used. In track and field, there is just the high jump event, though, in the past, there was also a standing high jump at the Olympics. There are also records for the vertical jump, running vertical jump, and the platform jump.

The standing high jump was an Olympic Track and Field event between 1900 and 1912. Unlike the conventional high jump event, part of the current track and field program, the standing version does not allow any run-up. The technique is performed from a position with both feet together. A champion in this discipline, Ray Ewry won the standing high jump (and the standing long jump) in 1900, 1904, 1906, and 1908. He set the world record for the standing high jump of 1.65 m on July 16, 1900.

Running High Jump events in track and field athletics have evolved as the technique and equipment have improved over the years. Significant changes occurred when the landing pit of sand or sawdust was replaced with foam mats, and the 'Fosbury Flop' backover technique popularized and perfected by American athlete, Dick Fosbury, was utilized in the 1968 Summer Olympics in Mexico. Here are the progressions for the men's high jump world record.

The high jump world record is 2.45 meters (8 ft 0.46 in), by Javier Sotomayor of Cuba, who achieved this height on July 27, 1993, in Salamanca (see High Jump Record videos).

Sotomayor also holds the indoor world record of 2.43 meters (7 ft 11.67 in). His outdoor world record set in 1993 is the longest-standing in the history of the men's high jump. (Ref 5)

While human vertical jump capabilities are impressive, various species exhibit extraordinary jumping abilities relative to their size. Fleas, for example, are known for their incredible jumping prowess. Fleas can jump vertically to heights more than 100 times their body length thanks to the unique structure of their hind legs, which contain a special protein called resilin that stores and releases energy, enhancing their jumping efficiency.

Landing Mechanics and Injury Prevention

When it comes to understanding the human body's movements, exploring the forces and motion involved is crucial. One area that requires careful examination is landing mechanics and injury prevention. Landing mechanics refer to how our bodies respond when we land after a jump or a fall.

It involves coordinating various body parts, muscles, and joints to absorb the impact and maintain stability. Proper landing mechanics are vital to preventing injuries, especially in jumping and other dynamic movements.

Landing mechanics refer to how our bodies respond when we land after a jump or a fall. It involves coordinating various body parts, muscles, and joints to absorb the impact and maintain stability. Proper landing mechanics are vital to preventing injuries, especially in jumping and other dynamic movements.

Primarily, it is essential to understand the concept of force absorption. When landing, our bodies experience significant force due to gravity and momentum. This force must be distributed evenly across our joints to reduce the risk of injury.

Bending knees and hips upon landing helps distribute the force and absorb it efficiently. This way, the impact is not concentrated on a single joint, such as the ankle or knee, which could lead to sprains or fractures. Landing with proper body alignment allows for better stability and reduces the risk of injury. We can introduce exercises and activities that improve balance and body control, such as single-leg balance exercises or landing drills.

Incorporating these exercises into training routines can strengthen the muscles that maintain balance and stability.

Proper footwear and equipment are important in injury prevention. Different activities require footwear and protective gear to support the body during landing. For instance, sports involving jumping and running may need shoes with extra cushioning and ankle support. Choosing appropriate footwear and using protective gear can significantly reduce the risk of landing-related injuries.

Landing mechanics and injury prevention are vital aspects of biomechanics that teachers should address when teaching Physical Science to middle and high school students. By understanding the forces and motion involved in landing, our students can learn how to protect their bodies from potential injuries. Teaching them about force absorption, proper body alignment, and the importance of appropriate footwear and equipment will equip them with the necessary knowledge and skills to engage in physical activities safely.

Spotlight on Basketball

Biomechanics plays a multifaceted role in basketball, influencing training, performance, and injury prevention. By strategically applying biomechanical principles, players and coaches can fine-tune training routines, optimize movement efficiency, and mitigate the risk of injuries.

The continual progress in biomechanical research and technology promises further to refine our comprehension of human movement in basketball. This ongoing evolution empowers athletes to unlock their full potential, continuously pushing the boundaries of what can be achieved in this dynamic sport. In the captivating realm of basketball, where each jump, sprint, and shot carry significant weight, a profound understanding of biomechanics can be a game-changer. It serves as the scientific backbone of the sport, guiding us in playing more skillfully, preventing injuries, and elevating our overall performance.

- Since basketball demands a delicate balance of speed, strength, quickness, and accuracy, biomechanics plays a pivotal role in unraveling its intricacies. Each dribble, pass, jump, and shot involves a myriad of intricate movements. Understanding biomechanics in basketball proves indispensable, guiding players to shoot more accurately, jump higher, run faster, and reduce the likelihood of injuries. Coaches and players can refine their techniques by deconstructing player movements and scrutinizing the forces at play. For instance, a detailed examination of shooting mechanics allows for determining the optimal angle and force, leading to improved basket success rates.

Twenty Intriguing Biomechanical Insights into Basketball

Fundamental Focus: Biomechanics in basketball centers around comprehending the intricacies of human movement within the sport's dynamic framework.

Key Components: The pillars of basketball biomechanics encompass kinematics, kinetics, muscle mechanics, and the detailed examination of forces and torques.

Shooting Precision: Shooting a basketball demands a meticulous and concentrated motion, contrasting with the swifter release and reduced force involved in passing.

Segmental Analysis: Kinematics, crucial in biomechanics, dissects the motion of body segments, offering insights into arm and leg movements during various basketball actions.

Power Source: The hip joint emerges as a pivotal element for generating power, especially evident in the mechanics of a basketball jump shot.

Strategic Leverage: Leveraging body positioning and timing becomes a strategic application in basketball biomechanics, notably observed during rebounding maneuvers.

Height Dynamics: A player's height significantly influences biomechanics, impacting reach, center of mass, and the utilization of leverage during gameplay.

Dribbling Expertise: Biomechanical prowess in effective dribbling hinges on factors like precise hand placement, adept ball control, and the rapid execution of movements.

Optimal Posture: The ideal body posture for a basketball player involves a low center of gravity, bent knees, and a straight back—a combination optimized for biomechanical efficiency.

<u>Sprinting Force:</u> Muscle contractions play a pivotal role in generating the force essential for swift sprints across the basketball court.

<u>Release Dynamics:</u> The angle of release becomes a critical biomechanical determinant, influencing the trajectory, arc, and accuracy of a basketball shot.

<u>Proprioceptive Precision:</u> Proprioception, the body's awareness of its position and movement, emerges as a linchpin for balance and coordination in basketball.

<u>Strategic Passes:</u> A behind-the-back pass strategically leverages biomechanics, surprising defenders and altering the passing angle for enhanced effectiveness.

<u>Dunk vs. Lay up:</u> The biomechanics involved in a layup starkly differ from those in a dunk, encompassing takeoff angles, force exertion, and power generation.

<u>Footwear Influence:</u> Footwear becomes a biomechanical variable, impacting traction, stability, and shock absorption during the varied movements in a basketball game.

<u>Center of Mass Significance:</u> The center of mass plays a pivotal role in maintaining balance and stability, acting as a biomechanical linchpin during diverse basketball actions.

<u>Uniform Considerations:</u> Basketball uniform design should prioritize comfort, breathability, and freedom of movement, all while minimizing drag on the court.

<u>Rotational Insights:</u> Understanding rotational motion principles in basketball involves delving into spin, angular velocity, and angular momentum

dynamics.

Fatigue Factors: Biomechanics succumbs to fatigue, manifesting in reduced power output, compromised coordination, and delayed reaction times among basketball players.

Three-Point Challenges: Shooting three-pointers introduces biomechanical challenges due to the extended distance and heightened force requirements, demanding specialized skills from players. (Note 6)

Chapter 6: Biomechanics of Throwing and Striking

Principals of throwing mechanics:

Rowing is a fundamental human movement that is essential in sports and our everyday lives. Whether throwing a ball, a frisbee, or even a paper airplane, understanding the principles of throwing mechanics is crucial for optimizing performance and preventing injuries. What are the fundamental principles that govern the biomechanics of throwing?

One of the primary principles of throwing mechanics is force production. When we throw an object, we apply force to it to make it move. Our muscles, primarily in our arms and shoulders, generate this force. Proper technique and muscle activation generate maximum force while minimizing the risk of injury. Exploring the physics behind force production, such as Newton's laws of motion, can help students understand the relationship between force, mass, and acceleration in throwing.

Another principle to consider is the importance of body positioning and sequencing in the throwing motion. Proper body alignment and coordination are crucial for effective throws.

The sequential activation of different body segments starts from the legs and transfers through the hips, torso, and arms. This sequential activation ensures a smooth transfer of energy and maximizes the Efficiency and power of the throw. Maintaining balance throughout the throw helps to optimize accuracy and prevent injuries. Maintaining a stable support base and focusing on footwork, weight distribution, and center of gravity contribute to maintaining balance during throwing.

Biomechanical Analysis of Overhead Throwing

Overhand throwing is a complex motor skill that requires the coordination of multiple body segments and the precise timing of muscle contractions. Understanding the biomechanics behind this action can enhance our knowledge of human movement and its applications in physical science education.

When analyzing overhand throwing, several key factors come into play. The kinetic chain, which refers to the sequential activation of body segments, is critical. The motion begins with the legs, which generate the initial force through a push-off from the ground. This force is then transferred to the hips and trunk, which rotate to generate power. The energy is further transferred to the shoulder, arm, and finally, the hand, releasing the object being thrown.

The forces involved in overhand throwing can be broken down into two main components: linear and angular forces.

Linear forces are the push or pull in a straight line, while angular forces involve rotation around an axis. In overhand throwing, both types of forces are present. The linear forces generated by the legs and trunk contribute to the forward propulsion of the object. In contrast, the angular forces generated by the rotation of the hips and shoulder enable the release of the object with speed and accuracy.

Optimizing the biomechanics of the movement is important to ensure efficient overhand throwing. By analyzing the biomechanics of overhand throwing, students can gain insights into improving their performance in various sports, such as baseball, softball, or javelin throwing.

Striking Mechanics: Exploring Hitting Sports

Many athletes strive to master the skill of hitting a ball with precision and power in sports. Whether it is baseball, tennis, or golf, the ability to strike a moving object requires a deep understanding of striking mechanics and how forces and motion affect the human body's movements in hitting sports.

When players swing a bat, racket, or club, they force the object to strike the ball. The muscles in the body generate this force, and several key factors determine its effectiveness. One crucial aspect is the player's technique, which involves coordinating their body's movements to generate maximum power and accuracy.

Another critical element in striking mechanics is the transfer of energy from the body to the object being struck. This transfer occurs through a series of movements and joints known as the kinetic chain. The kinetic chain starts from the feet, travels up through the legs, hips, torso, shoulders, and arms, and finally ends at the point of contact with the object. Understanding this sequential energy transfer is essential for teachers and students to grasp the mechanics behind hitting sports.

Furthermore, the concept of leverage plays a vital role in striking mechanics. Leverage is the ability to generate greater force using a more extended, longer lever arm. In hitting sports, this can be achieved by optimizing body positioning, such as having the correct stance or grip.

Understanding how leverage affects striking mechanics can help students develop more efficient and powerful swings. Moreover, the role of timing cannot be overlooked in striking mechanics. Hitting a ball requires precise timing to contact the moving object at the right moment. This involves predicting the ball's trajectory, anticipating its speed, and adjusting the swing accordingly. Teachers can explore concepts like reaction time, hand-eye coordination, and spatial awareness to help students improve their timing skills. Using video analysis and motion-tracking technology, students can observe and measure variables such as bat speed, angle of impact, and body positioning.

Chapter 7: Biomechanics of Lifting and Carrying

Lifting objects is an everyday activity that involves various forces and motions, and understanding the mechanics behind it can help prevent injuries and optimize performance. The fundamental forces, such as gravity and friction, affect the body's ability to lift objects.

Various lifting techniques commonly used in everyday life and sports activities govern Efficiency and safety. Proper body mechanics, including body posture, alignment, and joint movements, should be considered while lifting objects to prevent strains, sprains, and other musculoskeletal injuries. Ergonomics is a career field dependent on biomechanics.

Load Carriage and Ergonomics: Effects of Weight

In biomechanics, one crucial aspect is investigating load carriage and its impact on human movement. Load carriage refers to carrying external weight, such as a backpack or a heavy load, which can significantly affect the body's biomechanics.

When individuals carry heavy loads, their posture, gait, and joint movements can be altered. The body naturally adjusts to the additional weight by redistributing forces and modifying movement patterns. Depending on how well they manage the load, these adaptations can benefit and harm the individual.

Proper ergonomics play a crucial role in load carriage. Ergonomics focuses on designing tasks, equipment, and environments to fit the individual, ensuring Efficiency, comfort, and safety. In the context of load carriage, ergonomics seeks to optimize the interaction between the body and the load, minimizing the risk of injury and maximizing performance.
When examining load carriage and ergonomics, it is important to highlight

the potential consequences of improper load management.

Carrying excessive weight can increase stress on the musculoskeletal system, potentially causing injuries such as muscle strains, joint pain, and even long-term skeletal issues. Additionally, improper load distribution can impact balance and stability, increasing the risk of falls and accidents.

Conversely, understanding the principles of load carriage and ergonomics can empower individuals to make informed decisions and respond appropriately to mitigate the adverse effects. By optimizing load distribution, using proper equipment, and maintaining good posture, individuals can minimize the risk of injury and discomfort while carrying heavy loads.

Injury Prevention Strategies for Lifting and Carrying

Proper Lifting Techniques:

Proper lifting techniques prevent injuries. Emphasize the importance of maintaining a neutral spine, bending at the hips and knees, and using the leg muscles to lift rather than relying on the back muscles. Encourage them to keep the load close to their body and avoid twisting or jerking movements, which can strain the spine and other vulnerable areas.

Carrying Techniques:

In addition to lifting techniques, proper carrying techniques are equally important. Encourage students to distribute their weight evenly, using both hands whenever possible. Utilizing backpacks with two shoulder straps instead of single-strap bags can help distribute the load more evenly, reducing strain on one side of the body. Furthermore, remind them to avoid carrying excessive weight, which can increase the risk of injury.

Ergonomics and Environmental Factors:

Workplace design, equipment setup, and the proper use of assistive devices can reduce the risk of injury. Encourage students to assess their surroundings for hazards, such as uneven surfaces or obstacles that impede their movements.

By equipping ourselves with injury prevention strategies for lifting and carrying activities, we can effectively develop lifelong habits that prioritize their physical well-being, ensuring they lead healthy and injury-free lives.

Chapter 8: Biomechanics of Sports Performance

Biomechanical Factors Affecting Performance

By unraveling the science behind human movement, we can identify how forces and motion affect the body's abilities and optimize training programs.

Primarily, forces play a pivotal role in sports performance. Newton's laws of motion provide a foundation for understanding how forces act on the body. Students must comprehend the concepts of force, such as magnitude and direction, and how they impact an athlete's performance.

Comprehending the role of forces is paramount, from the powerful force exerted during a sprint start to the subtle forces involved in balance and stability during gymnastics.

Each sport has unique demands, and understanding how biomechanics affect performance in these contexts can enhance students' understanding. For instance, the biomechanics of swimming involve minimizing drag and optimizing propulsion, while in weightlifting, the biomechanics of efficient technique and injury prevention are paramount.

Analyzing the trajectory of a basketball shot can help pinpoint the optimal angle for success, while studying the spin of a tennis ball can improve students' understanding of the role of angular motion in ball sports.

This knowledge will provide a solid foundation for further sports science studies and equip students with the analytical skills to improve their athletic abilities.

Common sports movements, such as throwing, have already been introduced that can be analyzed biomechanically. Whether it is a baseball pitch or a basketball pass, throwing involves a series of complex movements such as the wind-up, the release, and the follow-through. By studying the forces and motions involved in each phase, students can understand how to optimize their throws for maximum Efficiency and accuracy.

Revisiting basketball, one notices how many individual movements result in a successful outcome: a ball in the basket.

Whether a basketball player leaping for a dunk or a long jumper propelling themselves through the air, jumping requires a thorough understanding of biomechanics. The force-velocity relationship determines how much force can be generated during a jump and how quickly it can be applied.

By understanding these biomechanical principles, students can improve their jumping abilities and reduce the risk of injury.

By collecting and analyzing these everyday sports movements, coaches and students can gain insights that propel athletes to victory safely.

By integrating biomechanical analysis into their physical science curriculum, teachers can give their students a deeper understanding of how forces and motion affect the human body's movements. This knowledge can enhance their sports performance and instill a sense of curiosity and appreciation for the science behind human movement.

Spotlight on Soccer (Football)

In football, where precision and power can be the defining factors of success, biomechanics application takes center stage. The quest to maximize the free kick, a critical aspect of the game, becomes an intricate journey through the biomechanical principles governing each phase of this skill.

At the heart of this exploration is the understanding that the instep kick, a widely employed technique, is key to unlocking maximum accuracy and power during a free-kick. The biomechanical analysis delves into six major phases:

- Approach
- Support Leg & Pelvis
- Swing Limb Loading
- Hip Flexion & Knee Extension
- Foot Contact
- Follow Through

The approach, the initial stage of the kick, is a study of angles. Optimal momentum is achieved with an approach angle between 30° and 45°, a revelation derived from foot and ball velocity studies. The nuanced mechanics of the foot's interaction with the ground, generating braking and propulsive forces, play a pivotal role in building momentum.

Moving to the Support Leg & Pelvis phase, the non-kicking foot's placement becomes a crucial determinant of power. Newton's Third Law comes into play, emphasizing that a greater force applied to the ground translates to a more powerful impact on the ball. The positioning of the support foot, the flexion of the knee, and the stability provided by the pelvis, trunk, and arms collectively contribute to the athlete's balance and control.

Swing Limb Loading, Hip Flexion and Knee Extension form the subsequent phase, where elastic energy is stored in the kicking leg. The coordination of movements, including the flexion and extension of joints, sets the stage for the forceful downward momentum of the kicking leg.

The "soccer paradox" comes to light, highlighting the simultaneous flexor moment at the knee joint during its extension. The critical moment of Foot Contact brings forth the coefficient of restitution, dictating the energy transfer between the kicking leg and the ball. The intricacies of this phase, lasting a mere ten milliseconds, determine the acceleration and power imparted to the ball.

Weight shift and the follow-through of the kicking leg influence shot accuracy and spin.

The Follow Through, the final act, elucidates the type of shot that follows. A straight-axis follow-through yields maximum power, while a lateral movement introduces spin.

The duration of contact with the ball determines shot power and is a crucial factor in injury prevention, gradually dissipating kinetic and elastic forces.

As these biomechanical principles unfold in the context of the football free kick, the narrative underscores their applicability across various sports, such as Futsal, Rugby, American Football, and more.

In sports, where precision and power intersect, the biomechanical journey of the football free-kick serves as a beacon—a testament to how targeted analysis and training can redefine outcomes and elevate a team's performance on the pitch.

Chapter 9: Biomechanical Assessment & Measurement

Tools and Techniques - Biomechanical Assessment

In the field of biomechanics, understanding how forces and motion affect the human body's movements is crucial. Various tools and techniques have been developed to accurately assess and analyze these movements.

One fundamental tool used in biomechanical assessment is **motion capture technology**. This technology involves placing markers on specific body landmarks and using multiple cameras to track the movement of these markers in three dimensions, capturing the intricate details of human movement.

Force plates are another essential tool in biomechanical assessment. These specialized platforms measure the ground reaction forces produced during human movement. By standing or jumping on the force plate, individuals generate forces that are captured and analyzed. Teachers can use force plates to demonstrate the relationship between forces and motion, allowing students to observe and measure different forces in action. This hands-on approach enables students to grasp concepts more effectively and connect theoretical knowledge with practical applications.

Biomechanical **modeling software** is an invaluable tool that allows teachers and students to create virtual simulations of human movement. Using mathematical algorithms, these software programs calculate joint angles, muscle forces, and other biomechanical parameters. By manipulating these variables, teachers can explore how changes in forces and motion affect the body's movements. Furthermore, students can experiment with different scenarios and observe the resulting effects, giving them a deeper understanding of biomechanical principles.

Other tools and techniques, such as **electromyography (EMG)** and pressure mapping systems, can provide additional insights into biomechanical assessment. EMG measures muscle activity by recording electrical signals generated during muscle contractions. This technology can help teachers and students understand how muscles contribute to movement and how different exercises or movements activate specific muscles. **On the other hand, pressure mapping systems** measure the distribution of pressure between the body and a surface.

By incorporating motion capture technology, force plates, biomechanical modeling software, EMG, and pressure mapping systems, teachers can provide hands-on experiences and real-life examples to engage and inspire their students in the fascinating world of biomechanics.

Quantifying Human Movement

Measuring human movement using technology is crucial for analyzing and understanding the intricate mechanics of the human body. Various methods for quantifying human movement, including motion capture systems, force platforms, accelerometers, and electromyography, are designed to track and record the three-dimensional movement of objects, often used in biomechanics to capture and quantify the motion of the human body during various activities.

These systems use multiple cameras placed strategically around a target area. The cameras track reflective markers placed on key anatomical landmarks, allowing the system to reconstruct the movement in three dimensions. Advanced systems can capture intricate details, such as joint angles and trajectories, providing valuable insights into movement patterns.
Force platforms measure the ground reaction forces exerted by a person during

movement. This data is crucial for understanding how forces are distributed during walking, running, or jumping. Force platforms are usually embedded in the floor and equipped with sensors that measure the forces acting on them. When a person interacts with the platform, the sensors detect the magnitude and direction of the forces. This information is then used to analyze aspects like gait, balance, and the impact of forces during various movements.

Accelerometers are sensors that measure an object's rate of acceleration. In biomechanics, they are often used to quantify the accelerations experienced by body segments during movement.

Accelerometers detect changes in velocity over time. When attached to different body parts, they provide data on the acceleration and deceleration of those segments. This information is valuable for assessing the intensity and timing of movements, helping researchers and practitioners understand the dynamics of various activities.

Electromyography (EMG) is a technique for measuring and recording the electrical activity generated by muscles during contraction. It provides insights into muscle activation patterns and timing during movement.

EMG involves placing electrodes on the skin above the muscles of interest. These electrodes detect the electrical signals produced by muscle contractions. By analyzing these signals, researchers can identify muscle activation patterns, assess muscle coordination, and understand the timing of muscle contractions during different movement phases.

Applications and Integration: These tools are often combined to understand biomechanics comprehensively. For example, motion capture systems can be synchronized with force platforms to correlate movement patterns with ground reaction forces. Accelerometers and EMG data can complement each other to offer a more detailed picture of muscle activity and overall movement dynamics.

Once the measurement phase is complete, analyzing the collected data gives meaningful insights into human movement.

Hands-on Activities:
Quantifying human movement through measurement and analysis is crucial to teaching forces and motion in biomechanics. This section will provide teachers with various hands-on activities to reinforce the concepts and engage students in active learning.

These activities will allow students to measure their own movements, analyze the data collected, and draw conclusions about the forces and motion involved. Students will develop a deeper understanding of biomechanics and its applications by participating in these activities. Research in biomechanics plays a crucial role in advancing our knowledge of human movement and its impact on the body. Researchers can gather objective data to analyze and interpret movement patterns by utilizing biomechanical assessment techniques.

This data aids in identifying faulty movement mechanics and potential injury risks. For example, motion capture technology allows researchers to track joint angles, forces, and muscle activations during various activities such as running or jumping. This information helps develop strategies to optimize performance and prevent athlete injuries.

Biomechanical assessment is valuable in fields such as physical therapy, sports coaching, and ergonomics. Physical therapists use biomechanical assessment to evaluate movement dysfunctions and design personalized rehabilitation programs. By analyzing an individual's movement patterns, therapists can identify specific muscle imbalances or joint limitations and develop targeted interventions to restore optimal movement.

Sports coaches also benefit from biomechanical assessment to enhance athletic performance. By analyzing an athlete's technique during specific movements, such as throwing a ball or performing a golf swing, coaches can provide feedback and make appropriate adjustments to optimize performance and reduce the risk of injury.

Furthermore, biomechanical assessment is crucial in ergonomics, where it is used to design efficient and safe work environments. Understanding the forces and motions involved in specific tasks, such as lifting heavy objects or operating machinery, helps minimize the risk of musculoskeletal injuries in the workplace.

By incorporating the applications of biomechanical assessment into your teaching, you can give students a deeper understanding of forces and motion in biomechanics and introduce them to the exciting research world and its impact on improving safety and performance.

Additionally, you can highlight the practical applications of biomechanical assessment in fields such as physical therapy, sports coaching, and ergonomics, inspiring your students to explore potential career paths in these areas.

Chapter 10:
Applications of Biomechanics in Daily Life

Biomechanics in Ergonomics and Workplace Design

"Biomechanics in Ergonomics and Workplace Design" delves into the fascinating intersection between biomechanics and the design of work environments. This topic is particularly relevant for teachers training to teach Physical Science to middle and high school students, as it explores how forces and motion affect the human body's movements in the context of workplace ergonomics.

Ergonomics is the science of creating workspaces that optimize human performance, safety, and well-being. Understanding biomechanics is essential for designing ergonomic workspaces, as it involves analyzing the forces and motion that impact the human body during various activities. Ergonomics uses biomechanical analysis to inform the design of workstations, chairs, and tools to reduce the risk of injury and improve productivity.

When exploring ergonomics and workplace design, it is crucial to consider the physiological limitations of the human body. By understanding the biomechanical principles that govern human movement, teachers can help their students understand how poor ergonomics can lead to musculoskeletal disorders and other health issues.

Key biomechanics concepts relevant to workplace design include force, motion, and torque principles and how they influence human movement. These designers require insight into how different forces, such as compression, tension, shear, and bending, impact the body when performing various tasks.

The field of ergonomics, also known as human factors engineering, emerged during World War II as a formal discipline. The roots of ergonomics can be traced back to the work of a team of British scientists and engineers addressing issues related to the design of aircraft cockpits and controls.

One of the key figures in the development of ergonomics was Dr. Frederick Winslow Taylor, an American engineer who pioneered scientific management principles in the late 19th and early 20th centuries. Taylor's work laid the foundation for the systematic study of work processes and Efficiency, contributing indirectly to the development of ergonomic concepts.

However, during World War II, the formal discipline of ergonomics took shape. The British team, led by scientists such as Alphonse Chapanis and John Paul Stapp, focused on improving aircraft control design to enhance pilots' performance and well-being. This work marked the beginning of ergonomics as a distinct field that considers humans' capabilities and limitations in the design of systems, products, and environments.

After the war, the field continued to grow, and various professional societies and organizations dedicated to ergonomics were established. Today, ergonomics is a multidisciplinary field that draws on psychology, engineering, design, and physiology principles to optimize the interaction between humans and their environments, tools, and tasks.

Biomechanics in Rehabilitation and Injury Prevention

Rehabilitation is a vital aspect of healthcare that aims to restore functional abilities and improve the overall quality of life for individuals recovering from injuries or surgeries. Biomechanics plays a pivotal role in analyzing the forces and movements involved in various activities and designing personalized rehabilitation programs accordingly.

By comprehending how forces and motion impact the body's movements, they can effectively explain the importance of specific exercises or treatments during recovery.

Injury prevention is another crucial aspect that biomechanics can address. By studying how forces and motion affect the body, teachers can educate students on proper body mechanics, ergonomics, and techniques to reduce the risk of injuries during physical activities. This knowledge can empower students to make informed decisions and adopt safe practices in their daily lives.

Biomechanical analysis involves observing and analyzing the forces and motions of different sports or activities to enhance performance and prevent injuries. By teaching students how to break down movements and identify potential areas of improvement, teachers can foster critical thinking skills and encourage students to apply biomechanical principles to real-life scenarios.

Conclusion: Unleashing the Power of Biomechanics

Throughout this guidebook, we have delved into the fascinating world of biomechanics, unraveling the science behind human movement. By harnessing the power of biomechanics, we can empower our students to explore and appreciate the intricate mechanics of the human body.

By shedding light on the connections between physics and the human body, we have learned how forces can be categorized into different types, such as gravitational, frictional, and muscular, and how they all play a crucial role in our daily activities.

One of the key takeaways is the understanding that forces and motion impact our gross movements and our fine motor skills. By studying how forces affect the human body's movements, we can explain complex phenomena, such as how athletes perform incredible feats or how dancers execute graceful movements.

Furthermore, we have explored how biomechanics can be applied to improve human performance and prevent injuries. By analyzing forces and motion, we can identify potential risk factors and design interventions to optimize movement efficiency and minimize the risk of injuries. This knowledge is invaluable for our students, as it encourages them to think critically about their own movements and make informed decisions regarding their physical well-being.

As teachers, we are responsible for equipping our students with the knowledge and skills to navigate the world of biomechanics confidently. We can harness the power of biomechanics in our classrooms and gymnasiums. By incorporating practical activities, real-life examples, and interactive discussions, we can ignite our students' passion for understanding the science behind human movement.

In conclusion, studying forces and motion in biomechanics opens a world of possibilities for our students. By embracing this field of science, we can inspire the next generation to appreciate the intricate mechanics of the human body and apply this knowledge to enhance their physical abilities. Let us embrace the power of biomechanics and empower our students to unravel the science behind human movement.

References

The following references provide valuable insights into the science behind human movement. They can serve as useful resources for teachers training to teach Physical Science to middle and high school students, particularly in biomechanics' niches of forces and motion.

Hamill, J., & Knutzen, K. M. (2018). Biomechanical basis of human movement. Lippincott Williams & Wilkins. This book is a fundamental reference for understanding the biomechanical principles governing human movement. It covers topics such as forces, motion, and the mechanics of human body systems, providing a solid foundation for teachers to build upon.

Winter, D. A. (2009). Biomechanics and motor control of human movement. John Wiley & Sons. This comprehensive textbook delves into the intricacies of biomechanics and motor control, providing detailed explanations of the principles that underlie human movement. It explores the relationship between forces, motion, and the human body's response, offering valuable insights for teachers to convey to their students.

Hamill, J., & Selbie, W. S. (2014). Research methods in biomechanics. Human Kinetics. This resource focuses on the research methods used in biomechanics, providing teachers with a deeper understanding of how scientific studies in this field are conducted. It offers guidance on experimental design, data collection, and analysis, enabling teachers to introduce students to the scientific process in their lessons.

Cross, R., & McNitt-Gray, J. (2017). Applied biomechanics: Concepts and connections. John Wiley & Sons. This book bridges the gap between theoretical concepts and real-world applications of biomechanics. It explores how forces and motion impact daily activities, sports performance, and injury prevention, making it a valuable resource for teachers to engage their students with practical examples.

Knudson, D. (2019). Fundamentals of biomechanics. Springer. This textbook provides a comprehensive overview of the fundamental principles of biomechanics. It covers a wide range of topics, including forces, motion, muscle mechanics, and joint kinetics, equipping teachers with a solid understanding of the biomechanical principles necessary to teach Physical Science effectively.

Bousfield, Daniel. "Football Kick Biomechanics." Football Kick Biomechanics, June 18, 2015, footballkickbiomechanics.wordpress.com/

Robert Wood, "High Jump World Records." Topend Sports Website, 2008, December 15, 2023

(Wikipedia contributors. (2023, December 12). History of physical training and fitness. In Wikipedia, The Free Encyclopedia. Retrieved 08:42, December 15, 2023, from https://en.wikipedia.org

By referencing these authoritative sources, teachers training to teach Physical Science to middle and high school students can enhance their knowledge of forces and motion in biomechanics. These references offer valuable insights into human movement's scientific foundations, enabling teachers to impart this knowledge to their students clearly and engagingly.

Lesson: Bikes-A Lever Idea!

ENGAGE WITH A DEMONSTRATION: Keep it Simple!

A machine is a tool used to make work easier. Simple machines are simple tools used to make work easier. Compound machines have two or more simple machines working together to make work easier. Can you find examples of these simple machines on these complex machines? Levers, Inclined Plane, Wedge, Screw thread, Wheel; Wheel and axel, Pulley.

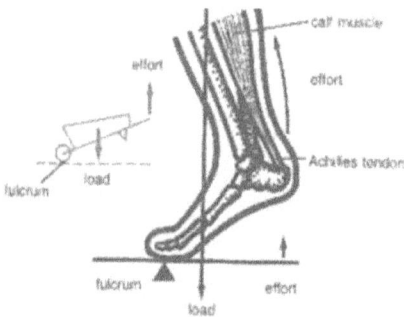

calf muscle

effort

effort

Achilles tendon

effort

fulcrum

load

fulcrum

load

effort

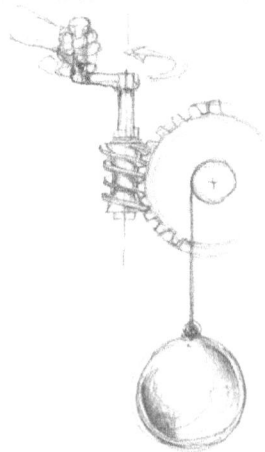

EXPLORE

Have students prepare to work in small groups (2-5).
Provide each group with a straightforward machine to examine in detail. Students should take turns operating the machine while the others watch to see how each part moves. Have students answer a series of questions to help them understand their machine.

What is the function of this machine?
How many moving parts does it have?
How are the moving parts connected?
What does each moving part do in the machine?

Place the machine so everyone can see it and distribute paper, pencils, and erasers. Students should begin sketching diagrams of their machines. Each student will see the machine from their point of view. Later, they can trade places and draw from different points of view to show all the working parts.

When the diagrams are completed, students should add arrows and written notes to indicate directions of motion for each part, label the elements of machines involved, and explain connections.

Have students display and explain their diagrams to other groups. Give each group a new machine to investigate and sketch if time permits.

EXPLAIN THE SCIENCE:

What are Simple Machines

A machine is a tool used to make work easier. Simple machines are simple tools used to make work easier. Compound machines have two or more simple machines working together to make work easier. Machines are used to multiply either the input force or motion, but not both, because even in. In the ideal situation of a frictionless device, the input and output work are equal. Because all real machines have some amount of friction, the input work must be greater than the output work; the ratio of (output work) to (input work) is always less than 1.00 or less than 100%, and this ratio is used to define the Efficiency of a machine.

The Mechanical Advantage of a machine is the ratio of (the distance moved by the input force) to (the distance moved by the output force or load); the Mechanical Advantage can also be calculated as the ratio of (load or output force) to (input force). In the device sketched here, the handle on the crank moves two hundred times as far as the load (the iron sphere being lifted); thus, theoretically, one lb. force applied to the crank handle will lift a 200 lb. weight. The machine, however, is not 100 % efficient, so slightly more than one lb. must be applied to the crank handle.

Mechanical Efficiency and Advantage of Bicycles: A Lever Idea

After more than 130 years of intense study and development, bicycles remain the most efficient human transportation machine ever manufactured. The biggest single improvement has been in tires, but the basic design concept remains unchanged. For hundreds of thousands of years, humans seldom traveled more than walking speed, 3 or 4 miles an hour. Runners can reach speeds of 20 mph for short distances, Olympic class runners can sustain 15 mph for 1 mile (4 minutes), but only an exceedingly small percentage of the population can run at 12 mph (5-minute mile) for more than a minute. Anyone reasonably fit can jog at 6 mph (10 min per mile) for a couple of hours or more. But in the 1890's, that suddenly changed with the "safety" bicycle. The average person could travel at 12 to 15 miles per hour for long periods (several hours). Professional athletes can maintain a pace of 30 mph for two hours or longer. A bicycle is a clever design of wheels and levers built around human anatomy.

The basic muscle actions are very closely those of climbing stairs or a steep incline. In some respects, a muscle is like a rubber band in that it only exerts a force in tension, which a muscle produces by contracting (getting shorter). The leg also resembles a linked pendulum system (a pendulum connected to a pendulum) but with significant constraints.

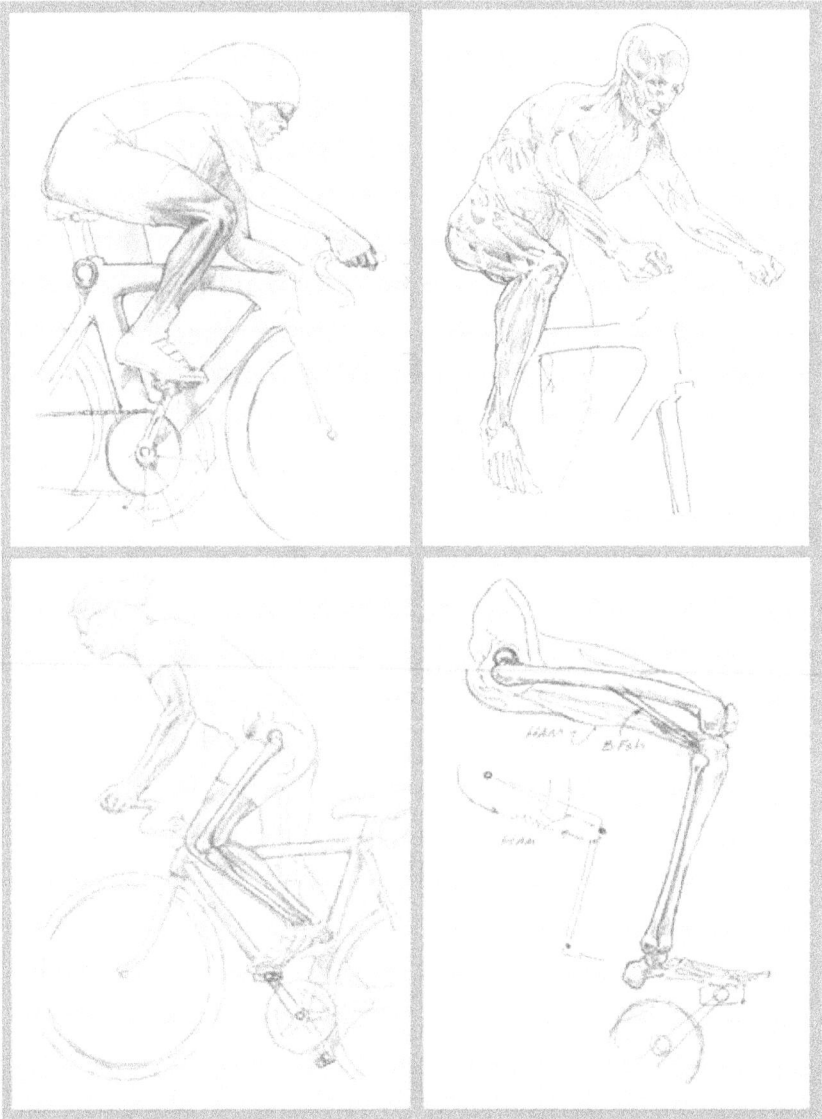

Any simple pendulum (a concentrated mass hanging from a string of length L) has a natural frequency, its period can be calculated from a formula first developed by Christiaan Huygens around 1659.

$$T = 2\pi \sqrt{\frac{L}{g}}$$

The average human upper leg (considering the femur as the pendulum length, L) has an approximate period (one full cycle) of around 1.3 seconds. The optimal pedal rate for racing cyclists is in the range of 50 to 60 cycles per minute, i.e., 1.2 to 1 second period. The muscles pull on the bones in the leg to set the leg in motion about its joints. Because the muscles are off-center from the joints of the bones, the tension in the muscles produces a lever effect about the joint, and the leg moves. There is a limit to the stress that muscle tissue can endure, about 44 psi or 300,000 N/m2; a load that generates greater tension in the muscle tissue may result in injury (a pulled "hamstring" being one of the more common ones). A modern bicycle and rider contain examples of all simple" machines but not necessarily in a simple isolated setting.

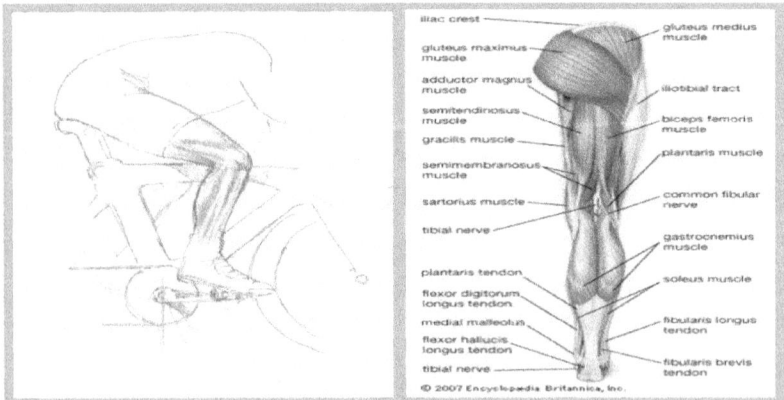

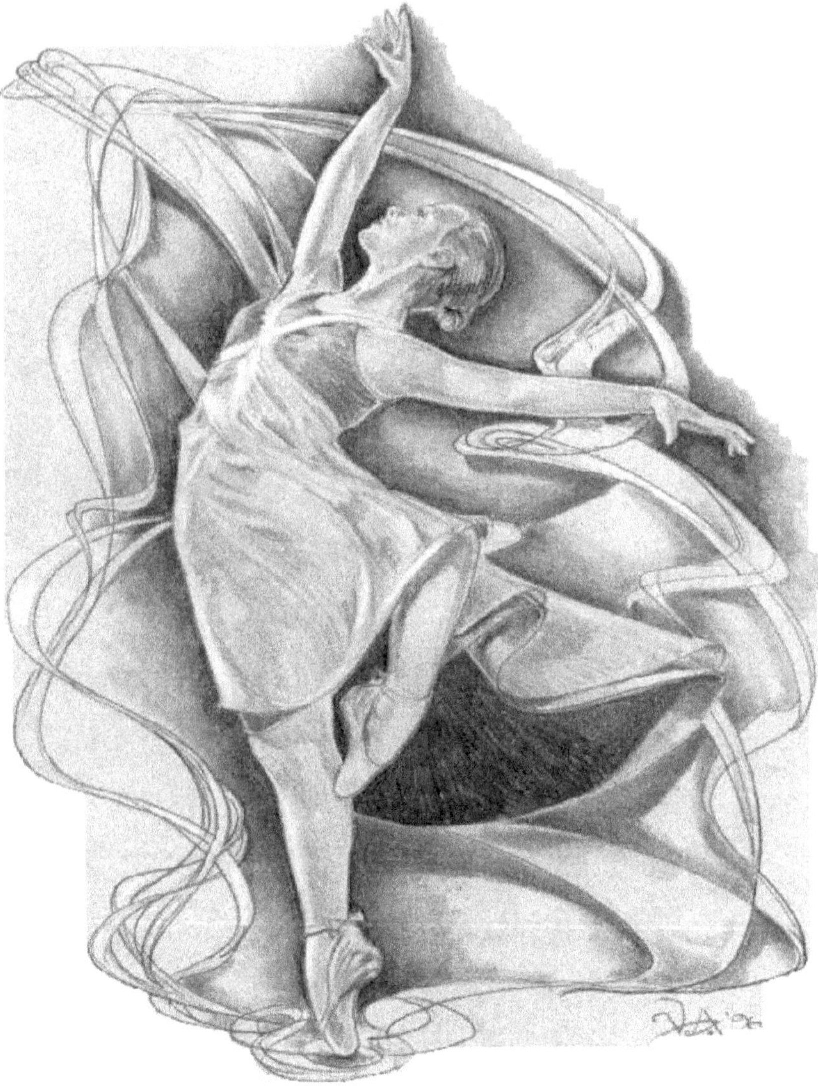

www.ingramcontent.com/pod-product-compliance
Lightning Source LLC
LaVergne TN
LVHW051153080426
835508LV00021B/2606